LEARNING TO IMPROVE YOURSELF:

Guide on how to improve while learning in less time

Alicia J.jenkins

Table of contents

Chapter 1

Understanding your brain to help you learn better

Understanding how the brain works will help you boost your results in any test. There's an obvious benefit to understanding why something works, and why you're learning.
This knowledge will help you utilize your brain more efficiently.
A brief tour of your brain
Imagine a cross-section of the brain, taken from the side.

The cortex is the biggest region of the human brain. It's connected with the higher brain function such as 'thought' and 'action', and is separated into 4 sections:
Frontal Lobe - involved with logic, planning, some speech, movement, emotions, and problem-solving

Parietal Lobe - involved with movement, direction, recognition, and perception of stimuli

Occipital Lobe – linked with visual processing

Temporal Lobe - involved with perception and identification of auditory stimuli, memory, and speech

Where your learning takes place

Learning arguably starts with Synaptic transmission, which is where neurons communicate electrical impulses.

The neurons never contact, and the spaces are filled with chemicals or 'neurotransmitters' which include dopamine and serotonin. These are commonly referred to as the body's chemical messengers.

Learning is forging new connections, remembering is retaining them

When this is repeated the link between neurons grows stronger and memory is established, and learning takes place.

How is this relevant?

It's significant since it demonstrates why repetition is so vital. So if you're reading something and it's not registering, you need to stimulate those neurons again - but potentially using new stimuli.

Try stating it out loud, or sketching a picture with the words. Keep researching possibilities to make it stick.

Your intellect isn't fixed

For many years we assumed that the brain, or intellect, was hard-wired, and mostly hereditary, with a set number of neurons.

But that all changed when it became feasible to study the brain and see how it reacted to what it saw and was asked to perform. This indicated that the brain can develop new cells - not just in infancy but also in maturity.

Knowing how the brain works might help you 'rewire' it. Evidence** supports the assumption that students who are conscious of how they learn will reflect on what they are doing. This naturally leads to the development of even more cells.

How our thoughts help us learn:

1. Understand that your brain is always changing. This implies that no one is locked at birth with a restriction on what they can learn. Instead, it's the belief in giftedness and how it affects the way instructors educate that hinders people's learning.

For example, when schools employ tracking—dividing children into various reading groups or math groups based on ability—it might create poorer outcomes for pupils than keeping mixed-ability students together. As research by Teresa Iuculano and her colleagues has demonstrated, the brains of individuals who have been branded early on as "learning disabled" may be rewired following a brief program comprising one-on-one tutoring.

2. Learn to accept hardship, errors, and failure. Pupils and instructors typically feel that achieving the correct answer on a test

proves that students are learning. But, as Boaler shows out, it's really when pupils practice tough things—problems just beyond their ability—that the brain works harder and imprints new information. This also makes the information more accessible later on.

Practicing what they can already do well actually hampers students' learning, whereas making errors helps them concentrate on alternative ways of evaluating an issue, which helps increase learning. When professors encourage students to struggle and students allow themselves permission to make errors, it can be extremely liberating for both.

3. Change your views about your mind, and your brain will follow. When you alter your thinking about yourself, it turns out that this will also transform your body and brain. For example, researchers showed that persons who had unfavorable beliefs about aging in

their earlier years—between 18 and 49 years old—were more likely to encounter a cardiovascular event within the following 38 years, independent of their beginning age, heart health, race, or many other characteristics.

The same is true for how you think about your learning. For example, if young kids learn that their success in school is tied to being smart rather than tied effort, they may be less motivated to learn later on.

4. Try several techniques to learn. Though it's crucial to have a growth mindset for learning—a notion that information isn't fixed, but can be improved through work and perseverance—it's also necessary to explore different learning tactics. Multi-dimensional methods of teaching and learning work best because they involve several parts of the brain at once, and communication between various brain areas improves learning. Even arithmetic

performance may be increased by apparently unrelated information or talents—like linguistic skills or finger perception (the capacity to recognize our fingers without looking at them) (the ability to identify our fingers without looking at them).

5. Aim for flexible thinking rather than quickness. Too frequently, instructors and learners assume that being quick at something indicates you're excellent at it. But, as evidence reveals, that's not typically the case. Trying to complete anything under pressure—such as a timed test—can generate stress, which affects the working memory required to retain critical information.

6. Try cooperation. Schools that teach a growth mindset won't necessarily help children learn better if there is no peer support for the idea—meaning if students still buy into the myth of the talented

student. Schools need to foster the concept that studying together is better than learning alone. As one research revealed, working together instead of alone may make the difference between passing a challenging math subject and giving up and failing the class.

Chapter 2

Cultivate the habit of reading

Reading is Part of Your Success
Education never stops, neither after school nor after attaining the career of your desires. Our life is a continual learning process, although some of us may not be aware of this.

how to regenerate the reading habit:\sThe desire to study and discover new things is one of the primary foundations when it comes to altering your habits and building healthy new ones. To better yourself, you should read frequently so that you may remain competitive in your profession by learning new tactics and strategies that differentiate you from others.

One step ahead is to reestablish the reading habit by reading high-quality books that strengthen your thinking, such as self-help non-fiction. When reading great non-fiction literature, your brain is coping with fresh concepts and ideas. Doing this regularly will teach you how to approach a topic from different aspects.

1. Place reading on your priority list

If you are busy and diverted throughout your work week, you should know that there is something you can do to remedy this. Turn your reading habits into concrete and time-sensitive objectives and set them on your priority list.

2. Find excellent books

Finding decent novels may be a tremendous struggle. In the beginning, you'll be prone to choice fatigue because of the huge quantity of books offered. This may sap your energies before you even began reading. To save effort in picking books, you might look for a curated selection produced by leaders you like. You may also Google the "favorite books" of successful individuals you follow, ask people you like what they read, or just pursue your interests.

3. How to enjoy reading
To acquire high outcomes, you should respect and additionally like reading. You may start by choosing books that correspond directly to a particular interest or ability you'd want to improve, then establish a specified time each day you'll read. Depending on your interests, you may look for books linked to personal development, habit modification, healthy living, productivity, and so on.

4. Plan your reading habit
Identify one hour per day when you can minimize one or more of your time-wasting habits and then set a daily calendar reminder that blocks off that hour for reading. Alternatively, you may arrange reading during breaks such as lunch or supper, or in the early morning before heading to work. Find several books to start

reading and arrange them near your preferred reading area to view them readily.

Put a pen and a notepad on the stack of books so you may jot down any ideas you acquire from reading.
Set a basic timer to make sure you read for at least 20 minutes. Or start by reading 20 pages every day, representing around 30 minutes. Although it may seem modest, it adds up quickly, the volume grows louder as time goes on and you'll feel the difference.

Useful techniques to make sure you remain focused while reading:

Use an app to monitor your daily habit.
Keep a book at hand when you are on the road so you can occupy "wasted" time.
Turn off the television when there is not much fascinating to watch.
Track your reading behavior daily.

5. Read as much as you can

Of course, don't restrict your reading time to 30 minutes each day when you have more time. Read as much as you can. You'll find that your writing abilities also improve when you start reading regularly owing to the new ideas you acquire continuously.

6. Read early in the morning

A smart tip is to start your day by reading at least 20 pages in the morning, even if it means getting up one hour earlier. In the morning, your mind is fresh and your body is calm after resting, so it's the best period to invest in yourself. Remember that most habits with a major influence on your life never seemed urgent even though they were vital, so take a little effort to create huge improvements.

7. Separate yourself from your phone

I don't know your lifestyle, but I do know that most of you have access to fast satisfaction that you may select over reading.

It's pretty darn hard, and I'll be the first to confess I don't do as well as I'd want to. But for reading time, I have learned to do a much better job of leaving the internet behind.

When cracking open a book, I implore you to separate yourself from the internet. Leave it on the opposite side of the room. Go outside and don't bring the phone with you. Go to a separate room.

When it's away from you, it needs an additional walk-of-shame-style chore for you to give yourself the brain break you convince yourself you need after every paragraph, section, or chapter break. If you need the dictionary, fetch your phone (or a dictionary, certainly) and just promise me you'll be back as soon as you can.

But disconnecting oneself from the internet is easier said than done.

For me, I gave myself scroll breaks all the time even though I kinda-sorta-all-the-way-didn't-like how social media works. I did it anyhow. I didn't have any notifications while I was gone, or I had ones that I didn't need to know quickly. There are exceptions to the rule, but most days, whatever it is that occurred on your phone, social media account, or email (if anything at all) while you were reading, could most likely wait for you to complete that chapter.

You'd be shocked at how much you can move ahead in a book when you maintain reading the words in front of you instead of the ones on your computer.

8. Read a variety of different types of books at the same time

This one may sound a little loopy if you're not already a "reader," but trust me, you're not always going to want to dive into a big meaty chapter if you don't have the time for it.

Sometimes, you're going to want to dip your toe in regardless of whether you're able to complete the chapter or not.

This is where nonfiction comes in handy for me. It's often easy to dive into nonfiction books without the commitment of a full chapter. It's also easier to stop in the middle of a paragraph and resume it without having to reread too much the next time I pick it up.

Because of this, I prefer to have a boatload of various style books at the ready.

And lastly, audiobooks rule, especially for nonfiction. They can be narrated by some terrific voice actors (sometimes even the authors themselves), and it can feel like a podcast or like you're sitting there hanging out with them while you're doing dishes, vacuuming, holding your baby with one hand and patting their butt with the other.

Again, if you're getting the vibe at all from this post yet—making a habit is all about making reading easier on yourself.

Expanding your format choices is a wonderful way to achieve them.

9.Stop reading books that aren't encouraging you

This is a contentious view and everyone's opinion is different, so if you read what I'm saying and think, "Jame, please kick yourself in the pants," that's great, but hear me out:

A thing about books is that they take the same amount of time to read whether you don't like them at all or whether it transforms your life forever.

So give that book you bought a shot. No doubt. Maybe even keep reading on if you still have hope for it moving forward. But when you feel uninterested to return to it, don't return to it. You could be reading something that alters your worldview for the better, and you can always return to that book you gave up on later if you want to.

There is one caveat though: you have to finish some books. I'm confident you will if you keep making time for it, but if you are someone whose habit has become reading the first chapter and then abandoning your last ten books, well then maybe you need to finish that next one that you're digging. You'd be surprised at how awesome books are when you get the chance to see the full picture.

10. Be patient with yourself

I get paid to read, and I'm still slow at it. Some brains just work that way. And you best believe that when you leap into reading after not having done it in a while, you're going to go through the pages slowly and you may have to reread certain things.
Do you know what you should do in that case?
Go slow.
Recognize that all you can do is read one word after the other. As long as you aim to understand what's on the page and not just move through it to get it done, you're going

to exit this reading experience one book stronger than when you came in.

In the end...

You can make reading as romantic as you want (favorite couch, favorite coffee, favorite candle, whatever) or you can pull out your book or Kindle without the romance—to just permit yourself to read.

Chapter 3

Self learning

What is self-learning?
Self-learning is the activity of obtaining new information or a new skill outside of a structured classroom context. It normally incorporates a diverse variety of strategies that may help you build a capacity to teach yourself new things. People who employ self-learning approaches may pick their subject of study, design their research methods and choose the breadth of their learning process.

Self-learning enables you to continue to build skills and obtain technical information outside of the classroom or your job context. For example, it may help you create a new passion, learn a new language or achieve important abilities that can help you progress in your job.

What are the advantages of self-learning?
Here are some advantages of beginning a self-learning process:

Develop secondary skills for your career: You may utilize self-learning approaches to enhance critical abilities for the job, like organization and problem-solving.

Become more confident in your talents: By understanding how to teach yourself new ideas, you may drive yourself to apply your skills to new projects and overcome any difficulties you confront.

Choose your learning path: People who self-learn may select the stages to utilize for getting new information depending on their learning styles, schedules, or general preferences.

Learn at your own pace: Instead of utilizing a fixed curriculum, you may select the speed

of your learning process and tailor it to meet your tastes and objectives.
Related: Guide to Self Improvement (With self-learning practices:

1. Determine your learning style
People typically prefer to acquire new knowledge or a new skill utilizing diverse ways. By examining various learning styles and understanding your learning process, you may identify the most beneficial approaches and tactics for you.

Here are some sorts of learners to consider:

Social learner: People with this learning style like to learn in a group environment and process knowledge via collaborative conversation. If you're a social learner, you may benefit from locating other individual learners to examine diverse views on the same issue.

Solitary learner: These learners like individual studying in calm situations. If you're a solitary learner, you may benefit from thinking about your own beliefs and obtaining access to numerous sources of information to enrich your foundation of knowledge.

Visual learner: Individuals with a visual learning style learn more efficiently via seeing visuals, including photographs, video footage, and diagrams. If you're a visual learner, you may learn best using color-coded organizing materials and witnessing demonstrations of new topics.

Auditory learner: An auditory learner processes more knowledge via sound and music than through other media. If you're this sort of learner, you may flourish by constructing mnemonic devices to recall material and listening to recordings.

Verbal learner: Studies new skills by reading, writing, and speaking. If you prefer to learn through the written word, you may benefit from annotating your learning process and reading books about your chosen topic.

Kinesthetic learner: Understands new concepts through physical activity, especially by participating in a process using their body. For instance, if you're a kinesthetic learner you may prefer to learn new skills that involve movement, like pottery, or you may enjoy studying during an exercise session.

Logical learner: People with a logical learning style prefer learning information through clear steps and pattern recognition. If you're a logical learner, you may prefer using numerical data and an organized system when preparing for a self-learning process.

Reading/writing learner: Individuals who are reading/writing learners may prefer to gain new information by reviewing written materials and taking notes or writing about their thoughts and conclusions. They may utilize papers, books, handouts, and presentation slides to research and study a certain subject.

2. Find a purpose

Determine what you want to learn about and why you want to be a self-learner. Developing an interest in a subject might give the drive to begin the self-learning process. Stay conscious of what material attracts you during the day or choose a skill set you're interested in studying. Then, consider pondering on how this new information could affect your life right now and how you might intend to utilize it in the future. For instance, if you intend to master fiction writing, you may pick if you're interested in obtaining a publishing career or retaining it as a pastime.

3. Set appropriate objectives

Establish objectives for a self-learning process to help you concentrate your efforts. It may be beneficial to pick certain parameters so you can optimize the phases of your approach. For example, if you're studying a programming language like HTML, you may establish a goal to construct your website with particular functionalities utilizing the information you've gained. Having a particular objective might also help you create reliable benchmarks for measuring your learning progress.

4. Access your core strengths

Reflect on your main qualities, abilities, and talents. This technique might help you find several parts of a subject that most interest you. For instance, if you're learning how to utilize picture modification software for the first time, it may be good to evaluate what you already know about photography and any other products with comparable user interfaces. By establishing your basic knowledge, you may assist drive yourself to continue the learning process and enhance general confidence in your skills.

5. Determine a schedule
To establish an effective strategy, it may be good to construct an agenda for your self-learning sessions. Consider assigning yourself a set of attainable deadlines and estimate how long each activity could take to accomplish. Depending on your preferences, you can plan your sessions using a physical notebook, an informal to-do list, or spreadsheet software. If you schedule lengthier self-learning sessions, try studying for 40 minutes at a time with breaks in between to enhance your capacity to concentrate.

6. Study in a favorable atmosphere
Choose a location to study that best meets your interests and requirements. Pick a

setting that supports your enthusiasm to study and helps you retain your concentration. Try to bring resources that enhance your learning process and attention skills, such as a computer, notepad, writing instruments, or a snack. Some individuals benefit better from an organized office in their house, while others may prefer a public setting like a library or park.

7. Read books and scholarly articles
Find books and scholarly papers from professionals to obtain additional basic information. If you're learning about a new area, reading material from established experts may give an outline for the knowledge important to know and your educational trajectory. Check a local library for appropriate book titles or free online databases for academic publications. Ensure that your study materials are correct and up-to-date. It may be good to acquire information from a librarian or another

professional who can advise you on what resources to utilize.

8. Find educational media

If you're an audio or visual learner, you may benefit from accessing instructional material. Multiple streaming sites may contain tutorials and other clips about your topic that you can bookmark in an itemized playlist. You might also explore listening to podcasts, which you can listen to throughout your commute or other tasks.

9. Take notes while you study

Many learners might benefit from taking extensive notes when studying new information since this practice can help you remain focused and boost your understanding. For instance, you may highlight portions of an article, summarize the information you learn, or add topics or words to explore subsequently. This method may be very effective for recalling information from movies or podcasts.

Here are several note-taking strategies you may integrate into a self-learning session:

Mapping method: Visually arrange a text or piece of media by linking concepts via drawn lines. You may even color-code it and add a number system, depending on your preferences.

Outlining method: Use indents or dashes starting on the left-hand side of the page or screen to arrange the tiny aspects of bigger issues.

Charting method: If the material is chronological, mark essential facts on a chart using categories and columns. Depending on your preferences, you may sketch the chart on a piece of paper or use spreadsheet software.

10. Review materials on the same day
Choose a time to analyze the subject you learned over the next 24 hours. This technique may boost your memory retention, helping you continue in your self-learning trajectory. It may be good to study your content during a transitional period, such as waiting for a bus to come or an appointment to begin. You may also examine stuff in the evening before you sleep or the following morning before you address the next phase of your objective.

11. Organize information
Organize your research and other useful resources in a way that works for you. Some individuals may choose to keep information in a physical area, such as a file cabinet or folder, while others prefer to utilize a computer-based resource. As you manage your workflow and the material you study throughout a self-learning process, it's crucial to ensure that knowledge is accessible and organized logically.

12. Apply your knowledge

Practice what you learned or apply your skills to a scenario in your daily life. By immersing yourself in the work you've studied, you can measure how much you've learned and may remember more critical information in the future. For instance, if you're learning a new language you can practice with a colleague or friend who's currently more proficient. You could also begin a small-scale project, like helping a friend organize their desk area if you've been learning about work productivity.

13. Collaborate with others

If you're a social learner or otherwise benefit from a group setting, consider meeting other people who are in the same self-learning process as you. By doing so, you can articulate your knowledge and point of view to someone else, which may help you assess your progress and recall key information with more ease. You can also clarify facts with another person and share any useful resources. It may be helpful to find a specific community on social media or online forums for this purpose.

14. Reflect on your progress

Classroom teachers typically provide you feedback on your learning process, therefore it's crucial to offer oneself the same resource. Dedicate some time every week to reflect on your progress and create new process objectives. You may also assess if the self-learning process is helping you reach its intended aim and how you might apply what you learned to other aspects of your life. For example, learning new computer software may increase your productivity during other administrative or school-related tasks.

Chapter 4

Testing your brain so it can remember anything

Don't despair. If you do the appropriate things, you'll be ready to ace any test.

To pull this off, you'll need to:

Learn and utilize the finest study approaches.
Study every day in a planned approach.
Optimize your nutrition, sleep, and exercise routines.
Study methods
There are a few study approaches that you should learn. They are the spacing effect and surveying.

THE SPACING EFFECT
The quickest approach to absorbing knowledge is to employ the spacing effect, a study strategy that scholars have termed

"one of the most astonishing phenomena to emerge from laboratory studies on learning."

As you learn new things, your brain stores that knowledge in neurons. It then links those neurons to existing neurons that store information you already know, producing a network of relationships.
The trouble is that your brain can only create this neural network of associations so strongly in one session. That bears repeating—it is physiologically impossible for your brain to create neural connections strong enough in one day for flawless recall. That's why if you push yourself to study the same knowledge multiple times in one or two days, often known as cramming, you'll have a hard time remembering it even if you studied for hours.

Researchers have determined that it's considerably more efficient to introduce your brain to new knowledge and then wait at least a day before revisiting that same information. This allows your brain time to consolidate the connections it has previously established, which means it will be ready and physically able to create those connections stronger upon the second encounter.

For example, if you have an exam coming up in a week, it's far better to study your notes just once a day for those seven days than 30 times in one or two days. Even though you'll have studied many times less, you'll perform better because you worked with the way your brain naturally remembers knowledge.

SURVEYING
The second research approach is called surveying.
By employing the spacing effect and surveying, you'll be able to evaluate all the material hundreds of times. These many-spaced exposures will be crucial in

helping you remember what you need to know.

Surveying is a strategy to assist you to reduce all the facts into something more manageable. I'm assuming that you're attending courses while acquiring all this knowledge, but if you're not, simply apply this to your textbooks.

Read your allocated chapters and extra readings the day before class.

Highlight just the key material in your textbook or other readings that isn't already bolded, italicized, placed in a box, or otherwise highlighted. Also, do not highlight anything that's in the subject sentence of each paragraph (typically the first phrase of each paragraph that includes the primary concept of that paragraph) (usually the first sentence of each paragraph that contains the main idea of that paragraph).

Go to the lecture and take succinct notes by hand.

Make sure to have these notes available so that you may review them at the same time you study your chapters.

From now on, when you re-read your chapters, just read headings, subject phrases, any material that was stressed by the author, and any information that you marked. Finish by reading the chapter summaries as they neatly tie together all the topics discussed throughout the chapter.

Most of the main concepts in reading are in the headings, subject sentences, stressed text, and anything you highlighted.

For instance, a subject sentence generally includes the major concept of a paragraph, while the remainder of the sentences solely expound on and clarify that key point. So, if you have previously read the chapter in its whole, you should have a concept of what's in that paragraph, and by reading simply the first phrase in each paragraph, you'll be reminded of what else is in the paragraph.

By doing this, a chapter that would take you an hour to read may now take you just five to 10 minutes, enabling you to revisit it periodically, receiving those numerous spaced exposures that are so crucial to recollection.

Also, examine your lecture notes once each day with your required readings. Since you created succinct notes by hand, they shouldn't take long to read, and the spaced exposures will guarantee that you recall them fully before a test.

This go-through will provide your mind with a comprehensive initial exposure to all you'll need to know.

Now your emphasis must move to receiving your spaced exposures, enabling your mind to view the same information again and again, but with at least a day of separation in between each exposure so that your brain can solidify the neural networks and be ready to strengthen them.

Remembering formulas

Having taken multiple financial courses, I know how tough it may be to recall all the formulae and functions you'll need to understand.

By reading and rereading the textbook, coming to class, and completing your homework, you'll be learning how to perform them, but you'll still need to tap into the power of the spacing effect to fully recall them. That involves obtaining several spaced exposures to all the formulae and clear instructions about how to solve them.

My recommendation is to create a notebook in which you write your instructions for how to solve every formula and equation you need to know, followed by a couple of examples. Then, when you're studying your chapters using the surveying approach, also take the time to go through these instructions and look at the examples.

By thoroughly going through this notebook every few days for the next several months, the spacing effect will help you remember all the directions. Then, when you're in your examination, it will be like an open-book exam, since all the instructions will be right there in your memory.

Test yourself
After a couple of months of spaced exposures to all the textbook pages, lecture notes, and reviewing your notebook with directions for how to solve formulae, begin testing yourself every couple of weeks. Choose several sample problems from your assignment, build a test, and see how you perform.

If you aren't performing well, then you need more spaced exposures. If you're doing well, make sure you maintain receiving your spaced exposures so that the knowledge will genuinely be established.
Optimize your lifestyle

There are various things you may modify in your everyday routine that can greatly boost your capacity to remember information.

PROPER SLEEP

Studies have indicated that kids who go to bed at or before 10 pm average as much as a letter grade better than those who go to bed at midnight or later.

There are a variety of ideas as to why this works (optimal melatonin production being my favorite), but you don't need to delve into the weeds to make this work for you. Just make it a point to be asleep by 10 pm every night and try to get as close to eight hours of sleep as possible.

This is critical for your academic performance. Not only will it optimize memory storage, but being well-rested means you'll have better focus when you're studying.

Chapter 5

Ability to teach yourself anything

27 Principles to Teach Yourself Anything:

1. Theory is optional. Practical application is necessary. Constantly ask yourself if or not this new information will make you more valuable - both for helping others and for following your own ambitions. Practical application dominates the world. That's what's going to get you a job. It's what will earn you a promotion. It's what will get your concept off the ground. What will get you financed. It's what will earn you money. It's what will genuinely assist people. Feel free to study the theory too if that's your thing (at times it may be entertaining), but never at the price of learning what's truly useable.

2. Showing up is only the beginning. It's no longer enough to show up to class, complete the assignments and take the the

examinations. That's table stakes. This is as true for formal education as it is for life. You must be willing to take what you learn and test, experiment and apply it to things that matter to you so you can discover what genuinely works, what's useful and what's a waste. No one else can do it for you.

3. Put yourself in circumstances where learning is essential to live and prosper. If your career, hobby or interest doesn't force you to always study then something's wrong. Make it a necessity and you can't help but progress. Sitting around hammering a keyboard and receiving orders doesn't need many fresh ideas. Changing the world does. Take the correct risks and create the suitable atmosphere. * Thanks to Anne Samoilov for inspiring this one.

4. Learn who you are. Know your strengths, passions, flaws, abilities, gifts, values, experiences, achievements, failures. Dig into yourself and examine it everything. I've

spent the past 10 years going to school on myself and I'm just just begun. This is a constant. It's precisely why I designed the Live Off Your Passion eCourse. Becoming a self-expert should be an obligatory minor (if not major) for every university student.

5. Learn what you love. This is the next stage towards understanding oneself. Constantly pay attention to the things that interest you. Notice those persons who inspire and drive you to be a better person. Catch yourself fantasizing about the company you wish you would have founded. Find the chores and occupations that you get utterly lost in. Watch attentively.

6. Learn what you dislike. The "I hate to do" list may be just as potent as the "I love to do" list. Notice the things that make your hair stand up on end. Know which hobbies and persons make you want to puke. Avoid them like the plague. Society does not gain by you spending more time doing things you

detest or being better at things you stink at. That is not what improvement is about. It's about taking the best of you and making it better. The world will be better for it.

Don't take anything for granted. Go out and try it everything. I'm talking everything. This especially goes for those lessons, suggestions and "social norms" that seem completely ridiculous. If something tells you there must be a better way, there often is. Go out and discover it. Just because it was done one way for 30 years, does not mean it has to be done the same way tomorrow. In fact, the longer something has been practiced, the more it should probably be questioned.

8. Record everything. What you adore. What you despise. What you're excellent at. What you stink at. What inspires you. What depresses you. Every feeling and lesson, good and bad, write it down and understand how it's building your narrative and how

you can utilize it to better learn and apply moving ahead.

9. Be cautious who you learn from. My own rule is: once three trustworthy and respected individuals suggest something, I do it. The only issue with our new world of self-guided education is that there is more pure trash accessible to study than ever before. There are tsunamis of books being produced, blogs being established and courses being given today. By default this means the sheer volume of mediocre or simply awful material accessible is growing through the sky. Your time and your intellect are valuable. Find a means to filter what you eat.

10. Analyze every investment. This and the above go hand in hand. Our time is valuable and our money comes in at a close second. For every dollar and every hour you're investing, make sure you're receiving a return. That may be in the people you meet,

the companies you develop, the skills you learn, or anything that you ascribe actual worth to. You decide.

If more individuals analyzed their investment in education as they do the beautiful, pricey baubles they buy, I guarantee we'd have a lot fewer persons roaming around seeking for work with theory-filled credentials and a mountain of debt. In order for anything to be an investment, it must have a return. Keep your standards high.

11. Teach others. There is no greater indicator of actual knowledge than when you can truly assist and teach someone else the content. Give, give, give. The high is unbelievable. Yesterday morning I interviewed Simon Sinek (author of Start With Why) for Online Your Legend (it will be live in mid January!). He pounded home the essential notion that we are here to serve and aid others. Nothing makes us feel

better. Check watch Simon's latest lecture If You Don't Understand People, Your Don't Understand Business, for an additional kick in the ass.

You know things that others wish to know. Identify it and create a means to provide it. Use a blog, the online, a community organization, your family, whatever. Trade knowledge. If you can teach anything to someone else, chances are they can teach something to you too.

12. Build stuff. This starts from day one. If you are reading about how to write, then start writing. If you're being taught how to interview, they go locate some job positions. People significantly overestimate how much time them must spend studying before they start doing. The answer is precisely ZERO. The time you start learning is the moment you must start developing and testing.

13. Break stuff. Don't expect everything you construct to function. In reality, much of it won't. That's where the finest learning occurs anyhow — in the screw-ups and the failures and in what you do as a consequence. The Wright Brothers were reported to have taken five sets of components to every attempted test flight since that's how many times they'd fail before dinner. James Dyson went through 5,127 prototypes before he produced the first vacuum that didn't lose suction. The folks who break the most things tend to enjoy the greatest success.

14. Make money. Most individuals don't earn money from things that are enjoyable because they either assume it should take much longer or they never ask in the first place. What if you placed a price on your experiments from day one? I bet there's someone who will pay you. And it's not until you have a paying and pleased (or dissatisfied) client, that you truly start to

realize whether your ideas are worth a cent. Does it assist others and will they pay you for it? That's the final determinant of whether your thoughts and education have validity.

15. Efficient is not the same as Effective. Simply because you can hand address 1,000 envelopes in an hour, doesn't mean you shouldn't just use a template and print them off in five minutes. And just because you can print 1,000 envelopes in five minutes doesn't mean you shouldn't ditch the snail mail completely and go to YouTube, blogs or the web where you can gain some real leverage (although I'm a major admirer of the thoughtful hand-written message on the proper occasions).

For some reason we've gotten fascinated with efficiency. But that's the very thing that might be killing us. Being Efficient is doing things right. Being Effective means doing the correct things. There's a tremendous difference.

16. Most education occurs outside of the classroom. Useful goods don't get created within your four walls. Learning doesn't happen inside a 15-pound textbook. The rubber meets the road when we decide to step out of what's comfortable and actually start interacting with the real world. That's where the data, the improvement and the magic happens.

17. Explore. My finest education to date was the years I spent studying at the London School of Economics (in a hands-on learning atmosphere) and operating a small company in Sevilla, Spain. That transformed my perception of the world in a manner that I never could have thought about. It made all the difference. World travel needs to be a must for everyone. Drop a year of school if you have to to save money. It's that crucial.

Explore everything. Yourself. Others. Ideas. The world.

18. Connections are EVERYTHING. The people you encounter determine what you learn, what you believe and who you are. Constantly examine what connections best suit your objectives professionally and personally. Keep the finest and fire the rest. Everything amazing in the world exists because of the individuals who got together to make it possible. The universe starts and ends with your connections. This is really the next course and book I've already begun working on for all you (tentatively titled How to Connect With Anyone — more on that shortly) (tentatively titled How to Connect With Anyone – more on that soon).

19. Don't presume anything. You may learn your most effective lessons in the most strange of locations. Expect this. Search them out. Have fun with it.

20. What if everyone had it backwards? Every so often, sit down and ask yourself: What if everything I've been taught is entirely backwards? What if the pundits are wrong? What would that look like? Invert everything. If you believe you need a year of experience to achieve anything, think about what would happen if you began doing it with just a day under your belt. I'm not recommending you do it, but at least think about it. See what comes up. Ok, then maybe give it a shot. ;) After all, what's the worst that could happen...

21. Try every medium. Read books and articles, listen to cassettes and seminars, watch videos and presentations (TED Talks are a wonderful place to start), jot down ideas and tales. There are so many methods for us to learn. Find those outlets that resonate most. Focus your studies there, but then take in the others to flip things on their head from time to time.

22. Get in arguments. Perhaps "discussions" is a better term. With friends, with smart people, with experts, with everyone. Find people who will test your ideas. People who will challenge your views and help you see things from viewpoints you may have been blind to on your own. It's remarkable how confident we can be of things right up until someone presents a more persuasive response. Be confident enough to stand up for what you believe, but be open enough to realize when you're wrong.

23. Find folks who think you're insane. Don't just surround yourself with people who believe exactly what you believe. Whether you do, you'll never know if your opinions are actually objective. Adept friends, mentors and models are frequently good at fulfilling the position of devil's advocate. You want these individuals around. They make you better.

24. Seek out different ways of doing things. The internet world makes this infinite. There are a million ways to earn a livelihood, alter the world and benefit others. Notice all the ways individuals have been successful. Find the tools that suit you best. Devour them. * See the end of this article for a free PDF copy of over 30 of the greatest online learning tools I've discovered.

25. Everything is a lesson. Every person. Every experience. Every hardship. All of it is your instructor.

26. Nothing is certain. Beware of individuals who are excessively confident of themselves. There's frequently alternative methods. Don't be naïve.

And finally...

27. It never ends.

There is always more to learn. There's always more to uncover. The learning never stops. Never. I don't care what your age or stage is. If you're not learning, you're dying, literally. The decision should be quite apparent.

Develop a passion for studying as you would for anything else you enjoy. Learn the things that fascinate you and use them in ways that make you and others happy and you'll become hooked in no time. The only choice is to make studying a passion.

Chapter 6

Understanding your reading pace

Whether you scan a blog article, study papers for work, or browse through a book, you most certainly perform some sort of reading every day. But trudging through lengthy tracts of text may be time-consuming, psychologically draining, and bad for your eyes. If you want to read more quicker while preserving reading comprehension, check out these seven strategies.

1. Preview the text.
Viewing a film's trailer before seeing the movie offers you background and helps you know what to anticipate. Likewise, previewing a text before reading it prepares you to swiftly obtain a comprehension of what you're going to read. To preview a text, skim it from the beginning to the conclusion, paying specific attention to

headers, subheadings, anything in bold or big type, and bullet points. To acquire a large picture idea, peruse the opening and ending lines. Try to find transition phrases, analyze any visuals or graphs, and figure out how the author arranged the text.

2. Plan your assault.
Strategically approaching a book will make a great difference in how effectively you can assimilate the content. First, think about your objectives. What do you hope to learn from reading the material? Jot down some questions you want to be able to answer by the end. Then, identify the author's aim in creating the content, based on your preview. The author's purpose, for example, maybe to chronicle the whole history of Ancient Rome, whereas your goal is just to answer a question regarding Roman women's involvement in politics. If your purpose is more restricted in scope than the author's, prepare to merely discover and read the necessary portions.

Similarly, modify your method of attack dependent on the sort of information you're going to study. If you're going to read a thick legal or scientific work, you should generally intend to read particular portions more slowly and attentively than you'd read a novel or magazine.

3. Be aware.
Reading rapidly with excellent understanding takes attention and concentration. Minimize external noise, distractions, and interruptions, and be attentive when your thoughts stray while you read. If you discover that you're thinking about your next meal rather than concentrating on the text, gently pull your thoughts back to the topic. Many readers read a few phrases passively, without attention, then spend time going back and re-reading to make sure they comprehend them. According to author Tim Ferriss, this practice, termed regression, can drastically

slow you down and make it tougher to gain a large-picture perspective of the material. Whether you carefully and attentively study a document, you'll soon notice if you're not comprehending a piece, saving you time in the long run.

4. Don't read every word.
To boost your reading speed, pay attention to your eyes. Most individuals can scan in 1.5-inch chunks, which, depending on the font size and kind of text, generally encompass three to five words apiece. Rather than reading each word separately, move your eyes in a scanning motion, leaping from a chunk (of three to five words) to the next block of words. Make use of your peripheral vision to speed up around the beginning and finish of each line, concentrating on blocks of words rather than the first and final words.

Pointing your finger or a pen to each chunk of a word can help you learn to move your eyes swiftly across the text. And it will urge you not to subvocalize while you read. Subvocalization, or quietly reciting each word in your brain as you read, can slow you down and distract you from the author's primary argument.

5. Don't read every section.
According to Dartmouth College's Academic Skills Center, it's an old-fashioned misconception that students must read every part of a textbook or article. Unless you're reading anything incredibly vital, skip the portions that aren't related to your aim. Reading deliberately will make it feasible for you to comprehend the major themes of several works, rather than just having time to thoroughly read a handful.

6. Write a summary.
Your task shouldn't finish when you read the final word on the page. After you

complete reading, write a few words to explain what you read, and answer any questions you had before you began reading. Did you learn what you were hoping to learn? By taking a few minutes after reading to reflect, synthesize the information, and record what you learned, you'll cement the topic in your memory and have greater recall later. If you're a more visual or vocal learner, create a mind map summary or tell someone what you learned.

7. Practice timed runs.
Approaching a book deliberately, reading actively, and summarizing well requires practice. If you wish to enhance your reading speed, use a timer to assess how many words (or pages) per minute you can read. As you're able to read quicker and faster, check in with yourself to make sure you're pleased with your level of understanding.